THE BOND MARKET IN THAILAND

AN ASEAN+3 BOND MARKET GUIDE UPDATE

DECEMBER 2021

ASIAN DEVELOPMENT BANK

Notes:
In this report, international standards for naming conventions—International Organization for Standardization (ISO) 3166 for economy codes and ISO 4217 for currency codes—are used to reflect the discussions of the ASEAN+3 Bond Market Forum to promote and support implementation of international standards in financial transactions in the region. ASEAN+3 comprises the Association of Southeast Asian Nations (ASEAN) plus the People's Republic of China, Japan, and the Republic of Korea.

The economies of ASEAN+3 as defined in ISO 3166 include Brunei Darussalam (BN; BRN); Cambodia (KH; KHM); the People's Republic of China (CN; CHN); Hong Kong, China (HK; HKG); Indonesia (ID; IDN); Japan (JP; JPN); the Republic of Korea (KR; KOR); the Lao People's Democratic Republic (LA; LAO); Malaysia (MY; MYS); Myanmar (MM; MMR); the Philippines (PH; PHL); Singapore (SG; SGP); Thailand (TH; THA); and Viet Nam (VN; VNM).

The currencies of ASEAN+3 as defined in ISO 4217 include the Brunei dollar (BND), Cambodian riel (KHR), Chinese renminbi (CNY), Hong Kong dollar (HKD), Indonesian rupiah (IDR), Japanese yen (JPY), Korean won (KRW), Lao kip (LAK), Malaysian ringgit (MYR), Myanmar kyat (MMK), Philippine peso (PHP), Singapore dollar (SGD), Thai baht (THB), and Vietnamese dong (VND).

ADB recognizes "Hong Kong" as Hong Kong, China and "Korea" as the Republic of Korea.

Contents

Note: The chapter and section numbering reflect that of the *ASEAN+3 Bond Market Guide 2016 for Thailand*, and includes only the chapters and sections being updated.

Tables and Figures

Acknowledgments

The *ASEAN+3 Bond Market Guide for Thailand* was published in October 2016.[1] Since then, the Thai bond market has experienced some changes to cornerstone features and seen significant innovation related to instruments and methods of issuance. As such, an update of the original *ASEAN+3 Bond Market Guide for Thailand* has become necessary.

Interested parties will appreciate the information on changes in private placement types and their comparison, new instrument and issuance types, the introduction of the Bond Investor Registration, and changes to existing measures to avoid Thai baht speculation. Due to the Securities and Exchange Commission, Thailand conducting its regulatory guillotine initiative, it is expected that the regulatory framework for debt securities and, in fact, for the capital market as a whole, will change sufficiently to suggest a complete revision of the *ASEAN+3 Bond Market Guide for Thailand*, likely in the course of 2022.

The ASEAN+3 Bond Market Forum (ABMF) Sub-Forum 1 team wishes to thank the Bank of Thailand; Securities and Exchange Commission, Thailand; and Thai Bond Market Association for their inputs and review of this update note.

No part of this update note represents the official views or opinions of any institution that participated in this activity as an ABMF member, observer, or expert. The ABMF Sub-Forum 1 team bears sole responsibility for the contents of this update note.

This update note and those relating to other ASEAN+3 bond markets are available for download from *AsianBondsOnline*.[2]

December 2021

ASEAN+3 Bond Market Forum

---

[1] Asian Development Bank (ADB). 2016. *ASEAN+3 Bond Market Guide 2016 for Thailand.* Manila. https://asianbondsonline.adb.org/abmg.php#tha-2016.
[2] Asian Bonds Online. https://asianbondsonline.adb.org.

Abbreviations

ABMF	ASEAN+3 Bond Market Forum
ADB	Asian Development Bank
ASEAN	Association of Southeast Asian Nations
ASEAN+3	Association of Southeast Asian Nations plus the People's Republic of China, Japan, and the Republic of Korea
BIR	Bond Investor Registration
BOT	Bank of Thailand
COVID-19	coronavirus disease
DLT	distributed ledger technology
ESG	environmental, social, and governance
HNW	high-net-worth (investors)
ICMA	International Capital Market Association
MTN	medium-term note
PDMO	Public Debt Management Office
PP-AI	private placement for Accredited Investors
PP-HNW	private placement for high-net-worth investors
PP-II	private placement for institutional investors
SEC	Securities and Exchange Commission, Thailand
SF1	Sub-Forum 1 of ABMF
SLB	sustainability-linked bond
SSA	Segregated Securities Account
TBX	Thailand Bond Exchange
ThaiBMA	Thai Bond Market Association
THB	Thai baht (ISO code)
UBO	ultimate beneficial owner
USD	United States dollar (ISO code)

USD1 = THB33.897 as of 30 September 2021 (BOT selling rate)

Overview

A.   Introduction

The Thai bond market has not seen fundamental changes since the publication of the ASEAN+3 Bond Market Guide for Thailand in 2016.[3] Instead, the Securities and Exchange Commission, Thailand (SEC), other market institutions, and policy makers have focused on fine-tuning issuance types, adding instrument types, and embracing the potential of new technologies in line with regional and global developments.

Chief among the developments was the introduction of green, social, and sustainability bonds, and the most recent adding of sustainability-linked bonds (SLBs) in the Thai market (see Chapter III.B) supported by the underlying frameworks for sovereign and corporate bonds. The current regulations also allow the issuance of green *sukuk* (Islamic bonds). Issuers shall comply with relevant international standards and practices in addition to the regulations related to issuance and offer for sale of traditional *sukuk*. In the last 2 years, the Bank of Thailand (BOT), the Public Debt Management Office (PDMO), and the SEC introduced bond platforms utilizing distributed ledger technology (DLT), which is also referred to as blockchain, for both government and corporate bonds (see Chapter III.E).

The introduction of the so-called "blockchain bonds" was preceded by careful planning and successful industry engagement amid medium-term strategies developed by the regulatory authorities and implemented over a number of years. For example, the BOT issued a whitepaper in September 2018, *Project DLT Scripless Bonds*, detailing the intended outcomes and the roles and responsibilities of all parties involved in the issuance process. The BOT then facilitated the first issuance of government bonds on the new platform about 2 years later. For easy reference, an English version of the whitepaper is available from the BOT website.[4]

The BOT also introduced a Bond Investor Registration (BIR) concept in early 2021, which requires nonresident investors—as well as resident investors in a pending second phase—wishing to or already investing in the Thai bond market to register with the BOT to allow for the timely monitoring of investment flows and a better understanding by BOT of the nature and types of bond investors who are required to maintain dedicated securities account at the ultimate beneficial owner (UBO) level. Chapter II.M carries details on the BIR concept, as well as further adjustments by the BOT to the Measures to Prevent Baht Speculation.

---

[3] ASEAN+3 refers to the 10 members of the Association of Southeast Asian Nations (ASEAN) plus the People's Republic of China, Japan, and the Republic of Korea. Asian Development Bank.
[4] Bank of Thailand. 2018. *Project DLT Scripless Bond: Investing in Thailand's future Transforming the securities markets infrastructure with blockchain*. Bangkok. https://www.bot.or.th/Thai/DebtSecurities/Documents/DLT%20Scripless%20Bond.pdf.

To further support the professional bond market segment in Thailand, and also to ensure maximum investor protection for those who need it most, in 2018 the SEC reviewed its private placement scheme—then referred to as private placement to Accredited Investors (PP-AI), who are deemed professional investors in the Thai market—and distinguished the issuance of bonds between those to institutional investors and those to high-net-worth investors (HNWs), with specific distinctions relating to prerequisites and disclosure obligations. A practical comparison of the old and new issuance types can be found in Chapter III. In the process of reviewing issuance methods, the SEC also clarified the characteristics and requirements for public offers. In addition, the SEC added the ability for issuers to issue bonds under a program concept that same year, after having studied this option carefully. The program issuance comes with additional continuous disclosure obligations that are explained in Chapter II.G.

Given the impact of the coronavirus disease (COVID-19) and the need for all policy bodies and regulatory authorities to formulate an effective response to the pandemic, the SEC has also committed to what is described as a "regulatory guillotine" approach to regulation by carefully reviewing the entire regulatory framework for the Thai capital market—including the bond market—and streamlining existing regulations, devising new and needed provisions, and discarding prescriptions no longer needed for a contemporary capital market environment. The efforts and the envisaged outcome of this approach are reviewed in detail in Chapter X.B.

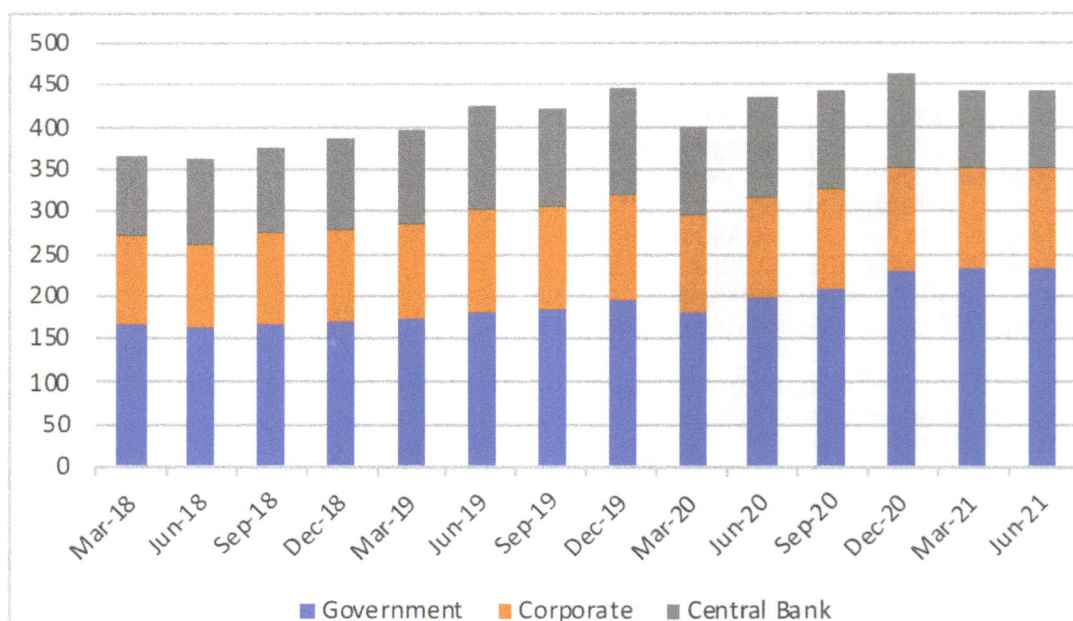

Figure 1.1: Local Currency Bonds Outstanding in Thailand
(USD billion)

USD = United States dollar.
Note: Data as of June 2021 and include bonds issued by nonresidents.
Source: AsianBondsOnline. Thailand Bond Market. https://asianbondsonline.adb.org/economy/?economy=TH.

Compared to the end of 2015, the last year referenced in the *ASEAN+3 Bond Market Guide for Thailand*, the total amount of local currency bonds outstanding had increased by nearly 60% by the end of June 2021, while corporate bonds outstanding alone had increased by 73% in the same period.[5] Government bonds continue to represent the largest segment of the market, with their share of total bonds outstanding increasing during the review period. This increase was due in part to the issuances of blockchain bonds and sustainability bonds in 2020, which have been widely accepted by domestic market investors (Figure 1.1).

In addition to bond market information available on *AsianBondsOnline*, comprehensive data on outstanding bonds and notes—and their issuance, composition, and trading volumes—as well as a breakdown by investor type are available on the websites of the BOT, PDMO, and the Thai Bond Market Association (ThaiBMA) (see Chapter VII for appropriate links).

B.   The Securities and Exchange Commission Strategic Plan, 2021–2023

As a result of the rapidly changing environment, the Thai capital market has encountered both opportunities and challenges. The SEC has developed the Strategic Plan, 2021–2023 (Strategic Plan) that considers all critical dimensions, including changing environments and the new era of finance, that present both opportunities and challenges for business sectors and regulatory agencies in Thailand's capital market. The Strategic Plan encompasses and integrates the country's 20-Year National Strategy, the National Economic and Social Development Plan, the Capital Market Development Plan, and the Ad-hoc Master Plan established under the National Strategy to address the COVID-19 situation.

The Strategic Plan retains the four goals and seven key strategies from the SEC's Strategic Plan, 2020–2022.[6] It also adds the goal of "recovery and strengthening" and the Ad-hoc Master Plan to ensure that capital market regulations do not impose impediments to—while providing tools for—businesses impacted by the COVID-19 pandemic.[7] Thus, there are five objectives and eight strategies:

1) building a capital market ecosystem conducive to sustainable development;
2) promoting financial well-being for the public through savings and long-term investment for retirement;
3) supporting growth and financing small and medium-sized enterprises and start-ups;
4) enabling a regulatory framework and international connectivity to enhance competitiveness and create opportunities;
5) implementing digital technology to increase the capital market's capacities and supervision;
6) enhancing supervision and effective enforcement in the Thai capital market;
7) ensuring systemic risk management in a timely manner; and
8) supporting liquidity enhancement tools for businesses affected by the COVID-19 crisis.

Additionally, to ensure that the strategy's objectives are met and the Thai capital market is propelled forward in a sustainable manner, the SEC has developed an agile and outcome-driven organizational plan by establishing strong foundations in three areas:

---

[5] Based on an analysis derived from the *AsianBondsOnline* data portal. Asian Bonds Online. https://asianbondsonline.adb.org/data-portal/ (accessed 16 November 2021).
[6] SEC Strategic Plan 20220-2022. Unofficial Translation. https://www.sec.or.th/EN/Documents/AboutSEC/strategicplan-2020-2022.pdf.
[7] The Strategic Plan, 2021–2023 is only available in the Thai language; the information relayed here is extracted from the Thai document and translated by the Sub-Forum 1 (SF1) team.

1) **Resilient workforce**. SEC employees are willing to assist with future initiatives.

2) **A responsive regulator**. The SEC possesses the information necessary to act proactively and ensure the continued stability and security of the information technology infrastructure.

3) **Service reform**. The SEC enhances public confidence in it by providing convenient and timely access to services.

Further, the SEC is implementing a regulatory guillotine scheme as part of its Strategic Plan to review existing laws and regulations in order to promote effective enforcement consistent with international standards and current circumstances. Laws and regulations that are no longer necessary, do not keep pace with changing circumstances, or continue to obstruct efficient market operations and development will be repealed or revised to alleviate the burden on relevant stakeholders.

As part of this scheme, the SEC recently concluded a public consultation on proposed amendments to debt securities regulations. The proposed amendments to the debt securities regulations are primarily concerned with the following: (i) reducing debt securities notifications to simplify rules and increase stakeholder convenience; (ii) reviewing regulations to ensure they are current and consistent with other types of securities regulations to avoid undue burdens on debt issuers; and (iii) revising regulations to make them more comprehensible, concise, and clear. More details of the regulatory guillotine scheme are discussed in Chapter X.

Meanwhile, relevant financial market regulators and industry associations have emphasized the importance of sustainable finance. The SEC issued regulations allowing the issuance and offering for sale of green bonds in late 2018 and social bonds and sustainability bonds in the middle of 2019. This was the first step toward Thailand's sustainable bond market development. In 2020, the Public Debt Management Office issued the country's first SLB to finance green infrastructure and social impact projects that support the country's recovery from the COVID-19 pandemic. To bolster the capital market's critical role in resolving social and environmental issues, and promoting the sustainable development of businesses across multiple industries, the SEC issued regulations in May 2021 governing the issuance and sale of SLBs. As with green, social, and sustainability bonds, the SLB regulations are based on internationally recognized standards and incorporate references to conventional debt securities regulation.

C.   The Bank of Thailand's Strategic Plan, 2020–2022

In the banking sector, the BOT's Strategic Plan, 2020–2022, which is themed "Central Bank in a Transformative World," identifies sustainability as one of seven strategic challenges that must be addressed effectively over its 3 years.[8] As a result, the BOT established four strategic directions for incorporating environmental, social, and governance (ESG) aspects into its operations:

- Embrace an organizational culture that always considers sustainability, including ESG aspects, in all of BOT's operations.
- Encourage financial service providers to embed the concept of sustainability, including ESG aspects, into their organizational culture and various aspects of their business conducts.

---

[8] The BOT's Strategic Plan, 2020–2022 is available from the BOT website at https://www.bot.or.th/English/ AboutBOT/RolesAndHistory/DocLib_StrategicPlan/BOT-StrategicPlan2020to2022-eng.pdf.

- Collaborate proactively with related agencies to mitigate the household debt problem and to reduce households' financial vulnerability.
- Support consumer protection in financial services and enhance financial and digital financial literacy. Promote financial discipline among the general public to strengthen their financial immunity and readiness for digital financial services.

Legal and Regulatory Framework

This chapter reviews the significant changes or updates to rules and regulations, regulatory processes, and other official prescriptions by regulatory authorities and market institutions in the bond market in Thailand since the publication of the *ASEAN+3 Bond Market Guide for Thailand* in 2016.

C. Legislative Structure

Table 2.1 has been updated for regulations with a focus or impact on the bond market that have been introduced since the publication of the *ASEAN+3 Bond Market Guide for Thailand*. Many of these new regulations will be referenced or reviewed in detail in the relevant chapters and sections of this update note.

Table 2.1: Examples of Securities Market Legislation or Regulations by Legislative Tier

Legislative Tier	Content or Significant Examples
Constitution of Thailand	Principles, Rights, and Obligations
Statutes and acts (key legislation)	• Bank of Thailand Act B.E 2551, 2008 • Securities and Exchange Act B.E. 2535, 1992 • Public Debt Management Act B.E. 2548, 2005 • Tax on Income from Debt Instruments Received by Mutual Funds (Amendment Act No. 52), effective 22 August 2019 [NEW]
Subordinate legislation (regulations, notifications, orders, and rules)	• Notification of the Capital Market Supervisory Board No. Tor Jor. 44/2556 Re: Rules, Conditions and Procedures for Disclosure regarding Financial and Non-Financial Information of Securities Issuers (Codified; effective 1 January 2014) [NEW] • Notification of the Capital Market Supervisory Board No. Tor Jor. 17/2561 Re: Application for and Approval of Offer for Sale of Newly Issued Debt Securities (Codified; effective 1 April 2018) [NEW] • Notification of the Capital Market Supervisory Board No. Tor Jor. 61/2561 Re: Offer for Sale of Debt Securities of Thai Government Agencies (Codified; effective 1 November 2018) [NEW] • Notification of the Capital Market Supervisory Board No. Tor Jor. 62/2561 Re: Offer for Sale of Bonds Denominated in Foreign Currency in the Kingdom of Thailand (Codified; effective 1 November 2018) [NEW] • Notification of the Capital Market Supervisory Board No. Tor Jor. 63/2561 Re: Approval Rules on Offer for Sale of Newly Issued Bond of Foreign Entity Denominated in Thai Baht (Codified; effective 1 November 2018) [NEW]

Legislative Tier	Content or Significant Examples
	• Notification of the Office of the Securities and Exchange Commission No. Sor Jor. 1/2564 Re: Rules and Procedures for Preparation of Factsheet (effective 8 January 2021) [NEW] • Notification of the Capital Market Supervisory Board No. Tor Jor. 31/2564 Re: Application for and Approval of Offer for Sale of Newly Issued Sustainability-linked Bonds (Codified; effective 16 May 2021) [NEW] • Guidelines on Issuance and Offer for Sale of Green Bond, Social Bond and Sustainability Bond [NEW] • Guidelines on Issuance and Offer for Sale of Sustainability-Linked Bond [NEW]

B.E. = Buddhist Era, denotes a year in the Thai calendar.
Sources: SEC, ASEAN+3 Bond Market Forum Sub-Forum 1 team based on publicly available information.

E.   Securities Issuance Framework for Debt Securities

The SEC adjusted the issuance types for private placements in 2018, aimed at improving the investor protection for HNWs and offering greater flexibility for offers to institutional investors. The SEC also introduced the ability to issue debt securities via a program, a feature that subsequently also became available to nonresident issuers wishing to issue both local currency- and foreign currency-denominated bonds in the Thai market. The more significant changes are reviewed in section F in this chapter as well as in Chapter III.E.

At the time of writing, the SEC was in the process of applying a regulatory guillotine concept, reviewing in its entirety the regulatory framework for the capital market, including for the bond market in Thailand. Some of the envisaged or expected changes to the regulatory framework are indicated in Chapter X.B.1.

F.   Securities Issuance Regulatory Processes

Notification of the Capital Market Supervisory Board No. Tor Jor. 17/2561 Re: Application for and Approval of Offer for Sale of Newly Issued Debt Securities (Codified; effective 1 April 2018); Notification of the Capital Market Supervisory Board No. Tor Jor. 61/2561 Re: Offer for Sale of Debt Securities of Thai Government Agencies (Codified; effective 1 November 2018); Notification of the Capital Market Supervisory Board No. Tor Jor. 62/2561 Re: Offer for Sale of Bonds Denominated in Foreign Currency in the Kingdom of Thailand (Codified; effective 1 November 2018); and Notification of the Capital Market Supervisory Board No. Tor Jor. 63/2561 Re: Approval Rules on Offer for Sale of Newly Issued Bond of Foreign Entity Denominated in Thai Baht (Codified; effective 1 November 2018) contained adjustments to the issuance types under a private placement. This affected the regulatory processes as well as disclosure obligations by issuers at the time of issuance and during the life cycle of the bonds. In addition, the SEC used the revised regulations to fine tune provisions for public offers.

Other SEC regulations revised at the time affected the issuance methods and regulatory processes for the issuance of bonds by nonresidents issued in Thailand and denominated in both Thai baht and foreign currency.

Details are mentioned in the following sections. Due to the ongoing review of the regulatory framework by the SEC, which is expected to result in further changes in the next 12 months, only significant changes to previous prescriptions have been included.

A complete description of regulatory processes for all issuance methods will be contained in a next version of the *ASEAN+3 Bond Market Guide for Thailand.*

1.   Regulatory Processes by Corporate Issuer Type

The SEC continues to apply the same regulatory processes for both nonfinancial institutions and financial institutions, other than with regard to the latter's capital requirements, within the same issuance method. However, the revisions in SEC regulations in 2018 further distinguished between the issuance methods; while public offers for sale require the full approval of the SEC and now come with additional qualifications for an issuer to be eligible, the approval for a private placement targeted at HNWs follows the registration of the transfer restrictions by an issuer, subject to the completion of the prescribed issuance documentation. Issuers may now also avail themselves of program issuance.

Significant differences are explained in the following sections.

3.   Issuance Process for a Nonresident (Foreign) Issuer

The issuance process as such for bonds issued by a nonresident issuer is the same as for a Thai issuer. An issuer shall submit an application for approval to the SEC to be eligible for issuing bonds to HNWs.

However, the issuance of bonds via a dedicated program has also become available to nonresident issuers following the concept's introduction by the SEC in April 2018. Please see Chapter III.E for a detailed explanation of the issuance program concept.

4.   Regulatory Process for Public Offers

Issuers wishing to issue bonds via a public offer for sale need to submit an application for approval to the SEC. In 2018, the SEC introduced specific criteria for an issuer of a public offer that it would consider when reviewing the application and giving approval (Table 2.2).

Table 2.2: SEC Review and Approval Criteria for Public Offers

Criteria	Thai Issuer	Foreign Issuer
i. The need to prepare financial statements in accordance with	Thai Financial Reporting Standards (TFRS) for Publicly Accountable Entities and audited by SEC-approved auditors	(a) TFRS (b) International Financial Reporting Standards (IFRS) (c) Financial Accounting Reporting Standards (d) United States Generally Accepted Accounting Principle (e) financial reporting standards recognized or specified by home regulator, or related laws and relevant rules of foreign country where its business has established, only if the foreign company has prepared and disclosed information in the financial statement with demonstrating effect

Criteria	Thai Issuer	Foreign Issuer
		of different item between such financial reporting standards and IFRS (reconciled IFRS) (f) other financial reporting standards recognized by the SEC Office.
ii. The issuer is not in the process of rectifying or having an ongoing obligation to comply with the Securities and Exchange Act B.E. 2535.	✓	✓
iii. Directors and executives will need to be listed on the database of directors and executives of securities issuing companies.	✓	N.A.
iv. Controlling persons shall not have any untrustworthy characteristics.	✓	N.A.
v. The issuer does not have a record of a material violation of the rules.	✓	✓
vi. The issuer has never violated against debt offering regulations for private placement.	✓	✓
vii. The issuer has no grounds to suspect that the disclosed material information is incomplete or inadequate or misleading.	✓	✓
viii. Directors, executives, and major shareholders may not be suspected of having interests in conflict with the best interests of the issuer's business or having benefits transferred from the business.	✓	✓
ix. The issuer may not be in default on principal or interest of any debt securities or in default on a loan payment.	✓	✓
x. The issuer may not be in breach of the terms and conditions of debt securities.	✓	✓
xi. The issuer does not have any record of the misuse of proceeds from debt offering.	✓	✓

B.E. = Buddhist Era (denotes a year in the Thai calendar); N.A. = not applicable; SEC = Securities and Exchange Commission, Thailand.
Source: SEC.

A fast-track approval process only takes 10 days to conduct due diligence and inform the issuer of any observation by the SEC in order to clarify such observation within the period specified in the notice of observation. The fast-track approval process is available for a listed company with an investment grade rating and without any issues in relation to good corporate governance. Otherwise, the observation period may take up to 30 days. In both cases, the SEC will notify the issuer of its consideration within 14 days after the clarification process has been completed.

The normal track regulatory process involves a 90-day observation period and 30 days for the consideration process.

The issuer will need to submit a registration statement and a (draft) prospectus and also produce a factsheet on the bonds to be issued, following the prescribed format for the factsheet amended by the SEC in 2021.

Issuers of a public offer may also utilize a program issuance for their offer (see Chapter III.E); in such cases, the issuer would have to file a supplementary form with the SEC if there were any significant changes prior to the issuance of each tranche. In addition, the issuer will have to submit a pricing form for each tranche, including the first issuance, for the registration statement to become and remain effective.

5.   Regulatory Process for Private Placements (PP-II and PP-HNW)

With the notifications mentioned in section F, the SEC distinguished and further clarified the issuance of debt securities through different types of private placement. The regulation became effective on 1 April 2018.

Instead of PP-AI, the SEC introduced private placements to institutional investors (PP-II) as well as private placements to high-net-worth investors (PP-HNW), both being subsections of AI.

Similarly to the previous PP-AI regime, the current PP-II are considered as a deemed approval, indicating the SEC's willingness to permit an issuer to initiate the issuance and offering process, provided the issuer complies with the respective prescriptions for an offering to institutional investors, such as the provision of terms and conditions and the submission of a registration statement compliant with the minimum requirements stated in the Securities and Exchange Act B.E. 2535, 1992 (SEC Act), as amended. The issuer of a PP-II will also have to formally register the transfer restrictions for the bonds with the SEC and indicate the same in issuance documentation and on bond certificates, if so applicable.

By contrast, offerings to HNWs are required to be approved by the SEC prior to commencing their issuance. The SEC intends to conduct a review of the application within 30 days from the date of complete submission; a fast track for applications on PP-HNW is not available. Additionally, such offerings impose additional disclosure requirements both before and after the debt securities are issued, including the use of clear and fair terms in the terms and conditions, and key financial ratios. The issuer of a PP-HNW will also have to formally register the transfer restrictions for the bonds with the SEC.

Clear and fair terms and conditions and key financial ratios are not required for offerings to institutional investors, as these institutions are deemed capable of understanding terminology and independently calculating and analyzing such financial ratios. Only bonds may be offered to HNWs under this regime, except where the issuers are commercial banks, finance companies, credit foncier companies, securities companies, or life insurance companies that can also offer short-term bills of exchange.

Appointing a bondholders' representative is required for PP-HNW offerings, but it is not required—or at least is not mandatory—for PP-II offerings. Similarly, an offering of complex products to HNWs must include a credit rating for the issue and, if applicable, a guarantor, whereas offerings to institutional investors are exempt from such requirements. Such information is not required, however, if the issuer intends to sell plain bonds, including floating-rate bonds—which are not structured bonds or have significantly different economic characteristics or risks—such as asset-backed securities. At the same time, issuers offering bonds to institutional investors may include credit rating information in the disclosure document if the investors agree and/or to attract a specific investor universe—such as prudential investors, including pension funds and insurance companies—that will only invest in debt securities with credit ratings.

For easy reference, a comparison of the main characteristics between the original PP-AI scheme and the issuance types PP-II and PP-HNW is provided in Chapter III.E.

G.   Continuous Disclosure Requirements in the Thai Bond Market

Notification of the Capital Market Supervisory Board No. Tor Jor. 10/2556 Re: Submission of the Registration Statement for an Offer for Sale of Debt Securities (Codified; effective 1 November 2018) and Notification of the Capital Market Supervisory Board No. Tor Jor. 44/2556 Re: Rules, Conditions and Procedures for Disclosure Regarding Financial and Non-Financial Information of Securities Issuers (Codified; effective 1 January 2014), as amended, introduced a number of additional disclosure requirements for public offers for sale as well as for the new private placement types. Details are mentioned in the following sections.

1.   Public Offers

Following the promulgation of the abovementioned notifications, an issuer of a public offer for sale will need to update a number of indicators on the debt securities through their tenor; these include the use of proceeds as well as key financial ratios published in the prospectus at the time of issuance.

If the issuer choses to issue a public offer via a program, the occurrence of a material event will have to be filed with the SEC (see also section 3 for details).

2.   Private Placements

Issuers having issued debt securities via PP-HNW are required to update the financial ratios in the issuance documentation on an annual basis; the issuer also has to report the use of proceeds and submit biannual financial statements to the SEC.

3.   Issuance via a Program

In cases when an issuer has opted to issue debt securities via a program, the 2018 regulations impose the need to notify the SEC during the tenor of the debt securities if any of a number of material events occurred.

In such an instance for a public offering, the issuer must promptly file Form 69-PO-SUPPLEMENT with the SEC and indicate if

  i.   the issuer suffers significant damage;
 ii.   the issuer discontinues all or a portion of its business operations;
 iii.   the issuer modifies its objectives or nature of business;
 iv.   the issuer enters into an agreement vesting other persons with management authority over the issuer in whole or in part;
  v.   the issuer enters into a joint investment, is a party to a merger or acquisition, or takes over another issuer or is taken over in accordance with Section 247;
 vi.   the issuer undergoes a business rehabilitation process;
vii.   an event in which the holders of debt securities shall raise the fact that the issuer is in event of default;
viii.   the issuer breaches the debt payment agreement (default);

ix.   the issuer materially changes its management structure or shareholding structure, or changes its directors, executives, or the person who has control over the issuer;

x.   the credit rating of debt securities has been downgraded;

xi.   the issuer's financial statements have a change in revenue or net profit more than 20% from the same period in the previous year;

xii.   the issuer increases or decreases its registered capital;

xiii.   the issuer changes its accounting policy;

xiv.   the issuer has a higher value of related party transactions than previously disclosed;

xv.   the issuer has significant investment plans;

xvi.   the issuer acquires or loses major commercial contracts;

xvii.   the issuer has a dispute that may cause the reduction of the shareholders' equity by more than 5%;

xviii.   the issuer increases the offering value of debt securities from those previously specified in the program by canceling or changing the resolutions of the Board of Directors or the resolutions of the shareholders' meeting that previously approved to issue debt securities under the program;

xix.   the issuer has changed the bondholders' representative and, if the bondholders' representative is a creditor, the issuer must disclose such relationship;

xx.   provide details on the offering of green bonds, social bonds, and sustainability bonds in Form 69-PO-BASE Part 3: Information about the debt securities project to be sold in Clause 2.1 (1) – (5);

xxi.   for the following items, add details or amend the information disclosed in Form 69-PO-BASE.
1. In the case of a green bond, a social bond, or a sustainability bond, complete Form 69-PO-BASE Part 3 with information about the bond project to be sold, Clauses 2.1 (1) - (5);
2. In the case of a sustainability-linked bond, complete Form 69-PO-BASE Part 3 with information about the bond project to be sold, Clause 2.2 (1), (4) and (5); (3) need only contain information about the issuer's obligations;

xxii.   the issuer has changed the external review provider for the offering of SLBs, as specified in Form 69-PO-BASE Part 3 information about the project debt securities to be sold, Section 2.2 (5) (in case the report has been submitted to the SEC Office, the information in the Form 69-PO-SUPPLEMENT shall be deemed to have been disclosed); or

xxiii.   the information on the issuer is materially different from the information disclosed in the first registration statement filed with the SEC and this has an impact on investor decision-making.

While the criteria for a notification to the SEC under the private placement scheme are principally the same as those for public offerings, criteria xiv. does not apply.

Under the private placement scheme, the issuer is not required to disclose the related party transactions (a waiver given by the accounting standard as a company does not offer securities to the public); the issuer is also not required to update the transactions.

I.   Thai Bond Market Association Rules Related to Trading, Reporting, and Registration

In its role as the bond market self-regulatory organization, the ThaiBMA adjusted a number of its regulations in the last few years, as detailed below.

Registration

The emergence of new debt instruments in the Thai market—including green, social, sustainability, and sustainability-linked bonds (SLBs)—prompted the ThaiBMA to issue Notification of the Thai Bond Market Association Board Re: Fee for Registration of Debt Instrument Information for Green, Social, Sustainability Bonds and Sustainability-Linked Bonds, which became effective on 27 March 2019.

To promote sustainable financing instruments, the notice waived the application fee and reduced the annual fee by THB10,000 per year. Unless rolled over, this incentive will be applied until June 2022.

Trading, Reporting, and Maintaining Trading Records

On 13 February 2020, the ThaiBMA amended the Notification of the Board of the Thai Bond Market Association Re: Standard Practices for the Bond Market (No. 2). It amended the notice of maintaining trading records to require members to create and maintain a tape or electronic recording of each trading transaction for a period of at least 3 months, or an extended period as stipulated by the SEC, to be promptly recalled and inspected by the ThaiBMA if so requested.[9]

J.   Thailand Bond Exchange Rules Related to Bond Listing, Disclosure, and Trading

On 29 December 2020, the Stock Exchange of Thailand (SET) published the Regulation of the Stock Exchange of Thailand Re: Cancellation of the Regulations of the Stock Exchange of Thailand and Revision to the Content of the Regulations of the Stock Exchange of Thailand in Relation to Debt Instruments which are Listed or Permitted for Trading on the Stock Exchange B.E. 2563 (2020).

This comprehensive regulation contained the notice of cancellation of, or amendments to, a number of SET regulations covering the listing and trading of debt securities on the Thailand Bond Exchange (TBX), clearing and settlement provisions, as well as related disclosure and membership requirements. The regulation became effective on 29 December 2020 in anticipation of the planned discontinuation of listing and trading of debt securities on TBX effective 1 March 2021 (see also Chapter III.L).

Details of the affected SET regulations can be found on the SET website.[10]

K.   Market Entry Requirements (Nonresidents)

A new market entry requirement for nonresident investors is the Bond Investor Registration (BIR) with the BOT, which is explained as follows.

---

[9] The ThaiBMA rules are available from its website at http://www.thaibma.or.th/EN/Rule/RulesEN.aspx.
[10] See https://www.set.or.th/rulebook/#/regulation/content/31538.

2. Foreign Investors

From 12 April 2021, foreign investors wishing to invest in Thai government or corporate bonds are required to undergo a BIR with the BOT; this includes existing investors in debt securities. The registration needs to be submitted at the UBO level and will be facilitated through the investor's custodian. To ease the necessary preparations by custodians and investors, the registration can be completed by 4 January 2022 at the latest.

Please also see section M.5 for details on the BIR.

M. Regulations and Limitations (Nonresidents)

This section reviews applicable changes in the Measures to Prevent Thai Baht Speculation reported on in the *ASEAN+3 Bond Market Guide for Thailand* and also details the introduction of the BIR.

3. Measures to Prevent Thai Baht Speculation

The BOT is implementing measures to maintain stability of the Thai baht. These measures have been refined and relaxed across some of the types of Thai baht transactions. The measures with direct relevance for the investment in securities, including debt securities are summarized below:[11]

a. Measures to Limit Thai Baht Liquidity

Domestic financial institutions are limited to provide Thai baht liquidity to a nonresident in the case of transactions undertaken without an underlying trade or investment in Thailand. Effective from 5 January 2021, the total outstanding balance executed by each domestic financial institution shall not exceed THB200 million per group of nonresidents, a reduction from THB600 million as reported in the *ASEAN+3 Bond Market Guide for Thailand*.

b. Measures to Curb Capital Inflows

Without underlying transactions, domestic financial institutions are limited in borrowing or undertaking transactions comparable to Thai baht borrowing from nonresidents. The total outstanding balance executed by each domestic financial institution shall not exceed THB10 million per group of nonresidents. This measure remains unchanged from the *ASEAN+3 Bond Market Guide for Thailand*.

c. Measure on Nonresident Baht Accounts and Nonresident Baht Accounts for Securities

Effective from 22 July 2019, Nonresident Baht Accounts and Nonresident Baht Accounts for Securities are both limited to an end-of-day balance not exceeding THB200 million per nonresident for each type of account, a reduction from THB300 million as reported in the *ASEAN+3 Bond Market Guide for Thailand*.

---

[11] **See** Measures to Prevent Thai Baht Speculation (bot.or.th).

This limit includes balances of all accounts of the same type opened by each nonresident across all domestic financial institutions in Thailand. Domestic financial institutions are not permitted to pay interest on accounts, with the exception of Nonresident Baht Accounts (time or fixed deposit) with maturities of 6 months or longer.

d.   Measures on Non-Deliverable Forward

Domestic financial institutions are not allowed to undertake non-deliverable forward transactions against Thai baht with nonresidents. This measure remains unchanged from the *ASEAN+3 Bond Market Guide for Thailand*.

5.   Implementation of Bond Investor Registration Scheme

On 12 April 2021, the BOT and the SEC launched the BIR, an electronic registration system for nonresidents investing in debt securities. The scheme requires that

i.   commercial banks providing custody services to arrange for their nonresident clients who invest in debt securities in Thailand must open Segregated Securities Accounts (SSA) at the UBO level and register for authentication with the BOT by 4 January 2022, and

ii.   the trading of debt securities must be settled through the SSA registered with the BOT only.

The BOT first advised the market of the upcoming BIR scheme in November 2020, as part of the publication of its plan to develop a new foreign exchange ecosystem for Thailand. The policy initiative contained four specific aspects, citing the BIR scheme as a measure under its intention to improve the monitoring and effectiveness of foreign exchange surveillance and management policy. The policy document is available from the BOT website. [12]

The primary objective of the BIR scheme was to obtain data at the UBO level and enhance data quality in terms of accuracy, coverage, and timeliness. The BIR will be implemented in two phases. The first phase started in April 2021 and applies to nonresidents, while the second phase applies to resident investors and will be announced in detail in late 2021. The BOT press release on BIR is available on its website. [13]

The SEC issued a corresponding regulation in November 2021 requiring SEC-regulated entities providing custodian, broking, dealing, and underwriting services to nonresident investors to arrange for their clients to register for authentication with the BOT under the BIR and to open an SSA account at the UBO level, similar to the BOT's requirements for custodian banks. In addition, the SEC will require debt securities broker–dealers to deal with nonresident clients who are already registered with the BOT. The regulation will become effective on 4 January 2022.

---

[12] See https://www.bot.or.th/English/MonetaryPolicy/MonetPolicyComittee/MPR/BOX_MRP /BOX4MPR_BOTDevelopFX.pdf.
[13] See https://www.bot.or.th/Thai/PressandSpeeches/Press/News2564/n2564e.pdf.

III

Characteristics of the Thai Bond Market

The additions or changes to Thai bond market characteristics are described in this chapter in the context of the existing structure of the *ASEAN+3 Bond Market Guide for Thailand*.

A.   Definition of Securities

4.   Definitions of Green and Social Bonds

In its Guidelines on Issuance and Offer for Sale of Green Bond, Social Bond, and Sustainability Bond, the SEC did not issue specific definitions of these instruments for corporate issuers but instead made reference to acceptable international standards and the definitions that these standards contain.

The Government of Thailand's Sustainable Financing Framework, issued in July 2020, included definitions for green and social bonds by setting the categories of assets in which the proceeds from bonds issued under the framework could invest.[14] These definitions are explained in the subsections below.

a.   Definition of Sovereign Green Bonds [NEW]

Green bonds are those debt instruments using their proceeds for one or more of the following investment categories, which are also further detailed in the framework:

i.   clean transportation;
ii.   renewable energy;
iii. energy efficiency;
iv.   sustainable water and wastewater management;
v.   environmentally sustainable management of living natural resources and land use;
vi.   terrestrial and aquatic biodiversity conservation; and
vii. commercial, public, and residential buildings (green buildings).

The framework also contains a list of project categories that are specifically excluded from use of proceeds for a debt instrument to be categorized as a green bond.

---

[14] The Government of Thailand's *Sustainable Financing Framework* is available in English from the website of the Public Debt Management Office at https://www.pdmo.go.th/pdmomedia/documents/2020/Jul/KOT%20Sustainable%20Financing%20Framework.pdf.

b.   Definition of Sovereign Social Bonds [NEW]

Social bonds are determined by the use of proceeds for projects in the following areas, with each area further explained in detail in the framework:

   i.   employment generation,
  ii.   employment generation (COVID-19 financing),
 iii.   healthcare,
 iv.   healthcare (COVID-19),
  v.   education and vocational training,
 vi.   affordable housing, and
vii.   food security.

The framework also contains a list of project categories that are specifically excluded from use of proceeds for a debt instrument to be categorized as a social bond.

B.   Types of Bonds and Notes

In recent years, the Thai bond market has seen the issuance of new instruments—including green, social, and sustainability bonds—from both corporate issuers and the government. In addition, innovative issuance types—such as via DLT—are likely to result in changes to the features and characteristics of bonds in the Thai market. Details on the new bond types and their characteristics are explained in the following sections, within the context of the structure established in the *ASEAN+3 Bond Market Guide for Thailand*.

1.   Thai Government Debt Securities

(ii)   Government Bonds

The Government of Thailand established its *Sustainable Financing Framework* in July 2020. Due to the comprehensive nature of the framework, separate or individual frameworks for green and social bonds had not been necessary. In addition, the government also issued government savings bonds for retail investors by utilizing a DLT bond platform.

(c) Sustainability Bonds [NEW]

Sustainability bonds are considered debt securities that combine the use of proceeds for green and social projects; there is no definition or specification for a particular composition of the two categories.

In August 2020, the PDMO issued its first sustainability bond in the Thai market, raising THB30 billion to finance green infrastructure and social impact projects supporting Thailand's recovery from the COVID-19 pandemic. The social projects included public health, job creation, and local public infrastructure development.

The sustainability bond issuance followed the publication of the *Sustainable Financing Framework* in July 2020.

(iii)   DLT Scripless Bonds [NEW]

BOT introduced a platform using blockchain technology for the sale and distribution of government securities in August 2020, starting with its retail savings bonds (see section E in this chapter for details on the blockchain platform).

The new technology platform itself did not change the nature of the debt securities issued or added specific characteristics. Bonds issued via the platform, which are referred to as DLT scripless bonds, are issued in scripless format but may be obtained as a physical certificate from the depository after the issuance, similar to the original savings bonds.

2.   Corporate Bonds and Notes

New instruments issued by corporates in the Thai market have included green, social, and sustainability bonds, as well as the latest addition to the sustainable debt universe, SLBs. These instruments do not necessarily differ in characteristics from traditional bonds. While green, social, and sustainability bonds focus on the use of proceeds from their issuance for specific eligible projects, SLBs come without such restrictions. Details are provided in the following sections.

(vi)   Green Bonds [NEW]

Thailand's first corporate green bond was issued offshore by TMB Bank in June 2018, denominated in US dollars and with an issuance volume of USD60 million. This green bond was issued to finance renewable energy, energy efficiency, and green building projects.

In the absence of binding domestic regulations for green bonds, and the issuance being prior to the implementation of the ASEAN Social Bond Standards, this initial green bond had been aligned to the Green Bond Principles established by the International Capital Market Association (ICMA). The issuance was supported by the International Finance Corporation, which also carried out the external review.

Green bonds issued since the initial issuance in 2018 have largely focused on renewable energy and low-carbon transportation; however, the issuance of sustainability bonds (see further below) also includes the use of proceeds for green projects, which may not necessitate the issuance of a green bond on its own.

At the time of compilation of this update note, there were 33 green corporate bonds registered with the ThaiBMA, including those issued by state-owned enterprises. Detailed information on green and other thematic bonds registered with the ThaiBMA is available from a dedicated webpage, as shown in section H in this chapter.[15]

(vii)   Social Bonds [NEW]

Corporate issuers have issued social bonds since October 2019, when the first bond aimed at women entrepreneurs was issued offshore by Bank of Ayudhya. The bond was aligned with the ASEAN Social Bond Standards and featured an issuance volume of just above THB7 billion.

At the time of compilation of this update note, there were four corporate social bonds registered with the ThaiBMA, all issued by state-owned enterprises.

---

[15] Thai Bond Market Association. Green, Social, Sustainability, and Sustainability-Linked Bonds. https://www.thaibma.or.th/EN/BondInfo/ESG.aspx.

(viii)   Sustainability Bonds [NEW]

The first sustainability bond from a Thai issuer was issued by a financial institution in October 2018 to finance green and social projects. The bond followed the ASEAN Sustainability Bond Standards and had a tenor of 5 years and an issuance volume of THB3.2 billion.

At the time of compilation of this update note, six sustainability bonds were registered with the ThaiBMA, including one issued by a state-owned enterprise and one denominated in foreign currency.

(ix)   Sustainability-Linked Bonds [NEW]

In July 2021, Thai Union Group issued the first SLB in the Thai domestic market, in accordance with the ICMA's Sustainability-Linked Bond Principles. SLBs typically carry returns linked to the specific target set by the issuer at the time of issuance (e.g., a shortfall in the targets will lead to a higher coupon payment for investors). Targets include ESG objectives.

SLBs issued in the Thai market are registered with and tracked by the ThaiBMA (see section H).

E.   Methods of Issuing Bonds (Primary Market)

Additional methods of issuing both sovereign and corporate bonds in the Thai bond market have been introduced since the publication of the *ASEAN+3 Bond Market Guide for Thailand*. In addition, the SEC has further adjusted the issuance methods for private placements.

1.   Methods of Government Securities Offering

The Government of Thailand added the issuance of government securities via a new blockchain platform to its existing issuance methods.

(c)   Blockchain Platform for Government Savings Bond [NEW]

On 26 August 2020, the BOT launched a new platform leveraging DLT for the issuance of government savings bonds. The platform is aimed at enhancing the investors' buying experience, improving operational efficiency, and reducing overall cost. The issuance via blockchain reduced the issuance timeframe from 15 days previously to just 2 days. The first issuance of government savings bonds amounted to THB50 billion and was sold within a week.[16]

The underlying initiative, known in the Thai bond market as the DLT Scripless Bond Project, aimed to apply DLT to develop a secure and efficient government bond infrastructure. It represented a collaborative effort among the BOT, PDMO, ThaiBMA, Thailand Securities Depository Co., Ltd., selling-agent banks, and the appointed technology vendor.

As part of the initiative, the use of DLT focused only on sales and distribution, as well as the registration functions, with application programming interfaces

---

[16] BOT. 2020. New Government Bond Infrastructure Launched with Blockchain Technology. Press Release. 11 September. https://www.bot.or.th/English/PressandSpeeches/Press/2020/Pages/n5963.aspx.

developed to connect to the traditional market infrastructure for cash payment, settlement, and safekeeping.

The PDMO sees this as a first step in the use of DLT and, following the success of the issuance via the blockchain platform, is planning to expand this issuance method to all types of government securities.

Please see section B in this chapter for more information on the characteristics of the bonds issued via the blockchain platform. A comprehensive description of the blockchain platform and the operational aspects of the issuance of DLT scripless bonds is provided in the project whitepaper published by the BOT. [17]

2.   Corporate Bond and Note Offering Methods

The SEC further adjusted the issuance types via private placements, to increase investor protection for HNWs and ease issuance requirements for institutional investors. In addition, the SEC introduced an issuance program concept.

Table 3.2: Comparison of Current and Previous Regulations on Different Types of Issuance and Offering of Debentures via Private Placement in Thailand

Qualifications	Previous Regulation (effective from 2012 until 31 March 2018)	Current Regulation (effective 1 April 2018)	
	PP-AI	II	HNW
Applicability	Bills and bonds	Bills and bonds	Bonds only
Approval	Deemed approval[a]	Deemed approval[a]	Filing of application for approval required (30 days for consideration)
Registration Statement	Yes[b]	Yes[b]	Yes[c]
Transfer restriction	Registration with SEC required	Registration with SEC required	Registration with SEC required
Key disclosure document	(Short) Prospectus[d]	(Short) Prospectus[d]	(Short) Prospectus[d]
Terms and Conditions	Yes[e]	Yes[e]	Yes[f]
Factsheet	Required	Required	Required
Credit rating	Not required[g]	Not required	Not required[g]
ThaiBMA registration	Yes[h]	Yes[h]	Yes[h]

[17] BOT. 2018. *Project DLT Scripless Bond*. https://www.bot.or.th/Thai/DebtSecurities/Documents/DLT %20Scripless%20Bond.pdf.

Qualifications	Previous Regulation (effective from 2012 until 31 March 2018)	Current Regulation (effective 1 April 2018)	
	PP-AI	II	HNW
Issuance under MTN program	N.A.	Eligible	Eligible
Bondholder Representative	Not required[i]	Not required[i]	Required
Issuance under AMBIF	Eligible	Eligible	Eligible
Post-Offering Obligations	Reporting required on 1. Sales results 2. Redemption or rights exercise(s) 3. Events that are material to the price or value of the securities 4. Updated financial statements	Reporting required on 1. Sales results 2. Redemption or rights exercise(s) 3. Events that are material to the price or value of the securities 4. Updated financial statements (annual)	Reporting required on 1. Sales results 2. Redemption or rights exercise(s) 3. Events that are material to the price or value of the securities 4. Updated financial statements (biannual) 5. Updated key financial ratios

AMBIF = ASEAN+3 Multi-Currency Bond Issuance Framework; HNW = high-net-worth investor;
II = institutional investor; MTN = medium-term note; PP-AI = private placement for Accredited Investors;
SEC = Securities and Exchange Commission, Thailand; ThaiBMA = Thai Bond Market Association.
[a] Deemed approval requires the registration of the transfer restriction (to II only) and compliance with any approval conditions.
[b] Registration Statement must fulfill minimum requirements under Section 69-70 of the Securities and Exchange Act B.E. 2535, 1992 (SEC Act), as amended, plus contain a factsheet.
[c] Registration Statement must fulfill minimum requirements under Section 69-70 of the Securities and Exchange Act B.E. 2535, 1992 (SEC Act), as amended, plus contain a factsheet and additional information i.e., specific risk of issuer, key financial ratios.
[d] Despite the names prospectus or short prospectus used in market practice or referenced in regulations, the SEC did not prescribe a particular form or format for PP-AI (and now IIs or HNWs), documentation, or disclosure items, but specifies the minimum content of such disclosure in Sections 69 and 70 of the Securities and Exchange Act B.E. 2535, 1992 (SEC Act), as amended.
[e] Terms and conditions must fulfill minimum requirements under the Securities and Exchange Act B.E. 2535, 1992 (SEC Act), as amended.
[f] Terms and conditions must fulfill minimum requirements under the Securities and Exchange Act B.E. 2535, 1992 (SEC Act), as amended, and the terms and conditions must be clear and fair to all investors.
[g] Credit rating required for complex products such as securitized products and perpetual subordinated debt. Credit rating is not required for plain debt securities.
[h] Applicable only to long-term bonds.
[i] Except for secured debentures.
Notes: Only issuance and offering types aimed at professional investors considered.
Sources: ABMF SF1 based on the Securities and Exchange Commission, Thailand and Chandler MHM.

(b)   Private Placement

Effective 1 April 2018, the SEC revised the issuance and offering of debt securities via private placement in relation to the original PP-AI concept into a distinction between offers to institutional investors and offers to HNWs.[18] Both types of investors had been part of the original definition of Accredited Investors (professional investors) published by the SEC in 2009. There was also a change in the definition of the private placement issuance type referred to as PP10 to limit the entry of individuals to the nondisclosure market.[19]

The revised scheme differentiates the approval process, credit rating requirements, and post-offering obligations for offers to institutional investors and those to HNWs. In addition, the latest scheme makes offers to both institutional investors and HNWs eligible to be issued under the medium-term note (MTN) program introduced by the SEC with effect from 1 April 2018. Details of any changes from PP-AI to the current private placement issuance and offering scheme are shown in Table 3.2.

(c)   Bond Issuance Program [NEW]

In April 2018, the SEC introduced the concept of a bond issuance program, colloquially referred to as an MTN program, for resident and nonresident issuers offering foreign-currency-denominated bonds and THB-denominated bonds in Thailand. From the date approval is granted by the SEC until the end of the program, the approved entity may offer plain vanilla bonds for sale to institutional investors, HNWs, and retail investors via public offering with an unlimited value and number of offers.[20] The approval period for a programmatic offering of bonds is 2 years from the date of the SEC's approval.

The approved entity must maintain its qualifications during the 2-year period in accordance with the following regulations:

- Notification of the Capital Market Supervisory Board No. Tor Jor. 17/2561 Re: Application and Approval for Offer for Sale of Newly Issued Debt Securities (Codified; effective 1 April 2018);
- Notification of the Capital Market Supervisory Board No. Tor Jor. 61/2561 Re: Offer for Sale of Debt Securities of Thai Government Agencies (Codified; effective 1 November 2018);
- Notification of the Capital Market Supervisory Board No. Tor Jor. 62/2561 Re: Offer for Sale of Bonds Denominated in Foreign Currency in the Kingdom of Thailand (Codified; effective 1 November 2018);
- Notification of the Capital Market Supervisory Board No. Tor Jor.; and 63/2561 Re: Approval Rules on Offer for Sale of Newly Issued Bond of Foreign Entity Denominated in Thai Baht (Codified; effective 1 November 2018).

Otherwise, the approved entity must rectify its qualification before the end of the 2-year period.

When applying for approval to sell debt securities to institutional investors and HNWs under an MTN program, an applicant may submit a registration statement on Form 69-II&HNW-BASE, which contains information about the issuer, risk factors, management structure and corporate governance, financial statements, and MTN program, among other things.

---

[18] Private Placement Scheme under the Notification of the Capital Market Supervisory Board No. Tor Jor. 17/2561 Re: Application and Approval for Offer for Sale of Newly Issued Debt Securities, effective on 1 April 2018.
[19] From 1 July 2021, PP10 can only be offered to directors, executives, major shareholders, and the affiliated companies of the issuer.
[20] Under the program, bonds offered to HNWs and retails investors are required to be rated as investment grade.

The SEC requires the submission of Form 69-II&HNW-PRICING for each issuance under an MTN program (including the first issue). This form contains critical information about each issue, including fact sheets, information about the proceeds, key financial ratios, subscription and allotment procedures, and a pricing supplement.

Nonresident issuers were allowed under Notification of the Capital Market Supervisory Board No. Tor Jor. 62/2561 Re: Offer for Sale of Bonds Denominated in Foreign Currency in the Kingdom of Thailand (Codified; effective 1 November 2018) and Notification of the Capital Market Supervisory Board No. Tor Jor. 63/2561 Re: Approval Rules on Offer for Sale of Newly Issued Bond of Foreign Entity Denominated in Thai Baht (Codified; effective 1 November 2018) to issue both foreign-currency-denominated and THB-denominated bonds through an MTN program. Similarly, nonresident issuers can issue an unlimited amount and number of offers on a private placement basis to institutional investors, HNWs, as well as retail investors for a period of 2 years from the date of approval from the SEC. During this period, the approved nonresident issuer must (i) maintain its qualifications in accordance with Chapter 1 Part 2 of the regulation, and (ii) maintain an investment grade credit rating if offered to HNWs or retail investors.

(d)   Corporate Bond Issuance using Blockchain Platform [NEW]

The ThaiBMA has explored the use of DLT under the SEC's regulatory sandbox, which aims to allow innovation testing in a closed environment. The participation of the ThaiBMA in the regulatory sandbox is expected to solve issues in the corporate bond market, such as the verification of bondholder ownership and the lack of interconnected data from individual bond registrars, which are time-consuming matters that can result in delays and inefficiencies in the bond issuance process. Under the sandbox regime, the ThaiBMA has set up a DLT-based bondholder data storage system, which will allow entities involved in the issuance and offering of bonds (e.g., investors, issuers, underwriters, registrars, depositories, and regulators) to access bond information more quickly and conveniently, experience a shorter book-closing process, and reduce the transaction time for bond trading in the secondary market.

Two issuers had participated in this regime at the time of writing:
(i) Toyota Leasing (Thailand) Co. Ltd., which issued a bond amounting to THB500 million and with a maturity of 11 months and 29 days that was sold to institutional investors and HNWs; and (ii) Kasikorn Bank, which issued a foreign-currency-denominated bond amounting to EUR17 million and with a maturity of 3 months that was sold only to institutional investors in Thailand. In testing to date, no technological issues have been found in the ThaiBMA system that could adversely affect investors.

This DLT project of the ThaiBMA under the SEC's regulatory sandbox is a major step forward and plays an important role in the implementation of the Thai Capital Market Digital Infrastructure, which was officially announced on 3 September 2019. This SEC initiative to develop digital infrastructure is expected to enhance efficiency and reduce costs for all market participants, facilitate equal access to financial services for investors of all sizes, and strengthen the competitiveness of the Thai economy.

H. Registration of Debt Securities

The requirement to register with the ThaiBMA also now includes the new instruments added to the bond market in Thailand in recent years such as green, social, sustainability bonds, and SLBs.

In fact, owing to the increasing significance of sustainable finance instruments, the ThaiBMA has dedicated a specific web page to these instruments (Figure 3.1).

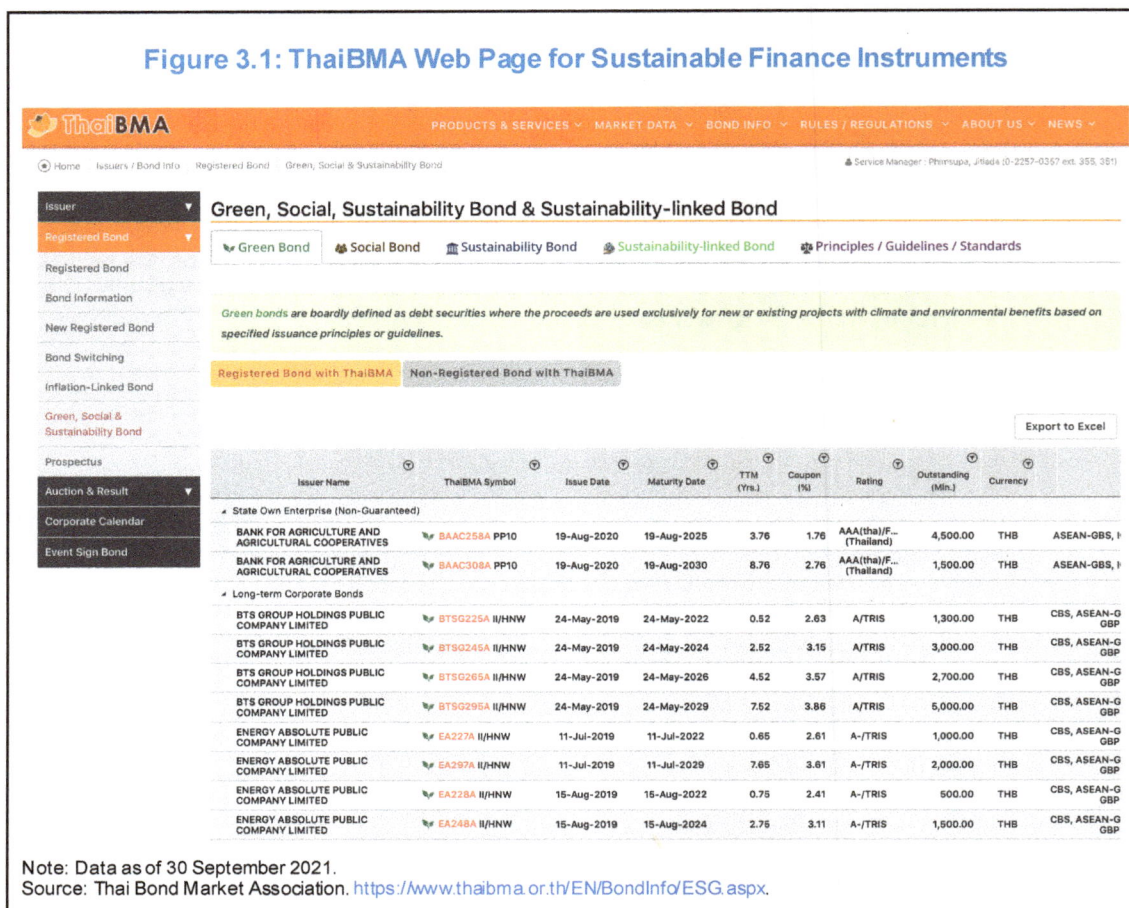

Figure 3.1: ThaiBMA Web Page for Sustainable Finance Instruments

Note: Data as of 30 September 2021.
Source: Thai Bond Market Association. https://www.thaibma.or.th/EN/BondInfo/ESG.aspx.

The webpage features individual tabs for each instrument type and also carries definitions for each instrument and the underlying principles or standards. Each list entry shows which principles or standards the debt securities are aligned with.

In addition to debt instruments registered with the ThaiBMA, the web page also offers a separate overview of instruments not registered with the ThaiBMA, for example instruments issued in a foreign market or offered exclusively to international development partners.

L. Listing of Debt Securities

1. Listed Securities

The SET, as an operator of TBX, announced on 4 February 2021 that the trading of debt instruments listed on TBX would be discontinued with effect from 1 March 2021.

At present, the ThaiBMA is the sole registration platform for bonds issued in Thailand (see also section H).

2.   Thailand Bond Exchange-Listed and Publicly Offered Bonds

The operation of the TBX was discontinued effective 1 March 2021, as such debt instruments are no longer listed or traded on TBX.

N.   Definition of Professional Investors

The definition of professional investors as such has not changed since the introduction of the concept by the SEC in 2012. However, the SEC has further aligned debt securities issuance types, particularly private placements, to specific investor types. The changes are explained in Chapter II.F.5.

At the time of the compilation of this update note, the SEC was in the process of reviewing the professional investor categorization and is expected to make further adjustments to individual categories and their eligibility criteria in the near future. Some of the envisaged changes to the professional investor concept are outlined in Chapter X.B.1.

Bond Market Costs and Taxation

Changes related to bond market costs and taxation detailed in this update note focus on the recent introduction of concessions as well as the most recent changes to tax rates and taxation practices in the Thai bond market.

Interested parties are encouraged to confirm the applicability of market rates, fees, and charges detailed in the *ASEAN+3 Bond Market Guide for Thailand*.

A. Costs Associated with Bond and Note Issuance

The Government of Thailand's response to the economic impact of the COVID-19 pandemic has included a number of concessions in relation to activities in the bond or capital market, which are described below.

2. Filing of Registration Statement or (Draft) Offering Circular with the Securities and Exchange Commission (mandatory)

Since May 2019, the SEC has waived registration fees for green bonds, social bonds, and sustainability bonds issued between May 2019 and May 2020. This incentive was subsequently extended and will now be valid until 31 May 2022. Following the issuance of the SLB regulation in May 2021, this incentive was also expanded to include SLBs.

3. Registration with the Thai Bond Market Association

ThaiBMA announced on 27 March 2019 that the application fee for green, social, and sustainability bonds issued pursuant to SEC regulations will be waived, with the annual fee reduced by THB10,000 per year, effective from 26 March 2019 to 28 June 2020. Similarly, this incentive was subsequently extended until June 2022 and expanded to include the SLBs.

G. Taxation Framework and Requirements

This section only covers changes in the treatment of investment income from debt securities for mutual funds. For other subjects related to taxation, please refer to Chapter VI.G in the *ASEAN+3 Bond Market Guide for Thailand*.

8. Investments in Debentures Through Mutual Funds

As of April 2019, investments in debentures by mutual funds established under the Thai securities and exchange law are exempt from income tax under the Revenue Code because mutual funds are juristic persons separate from fund management institutions. All benefits that mutual funds receive in interest, capital gains, and discounts are exempt from tax computation. However, unit holders of mutual funds are liable to income tax applicable to natural or juristic persons, as the case may be, on profit sharing of the investment units in the same manner as the tax liability of investments in equity instruments.

Nevertheless, the Amendment of Revenue Code regarding Tax on Income from Debt Instruments Received by Mutual Funds (Amendment Act) was approved by the National Legislative Assembly on 13 February 2019. The Amendment Act was subsequently published in the Royal Gazette on 22 May 2019 and came into effect on 22 August 2019, or 90 days after its publication in the Royal Gazette. The Amendment Act aims to equalize an effective income tax rate arising from debt instruments held by a direct investor and an indirect investor who invests through mutual funds by changing the mutual fund's status to a tax entity under the Revenue Code, prescribing a tax implication on the interest income of a mutual fund and improving tax implication on the mutual fund's investor.

According to the Amendment Act, the interest income of mutual funds paid from investments in debentures is required to be included for mutual fund's tax computation and is subject to a 15% income tax on gross income, provided that such debentures are received on the effective date of the Amendment Act onward. Gross income shall include only income as established under Section 40(4)(a) of the Thailand Revenue Code, such as interest income and discounts derived by the mutual funds. The income tax can be collected via a withholding tax mechanism applicable on the payment of such income by the issuer of respective debt instruments, resulting in issuers of debt instruments (which previously had no withholding tax obligations on payments made to mutual funds) being required to deduct a 15% withholding tax on such payments (similar to their withholding tax obligations already applicable on payments to other investors). However, it is worth noting that any tax withheld can be credited against the mutual fund's income tax payable and that it should not apply to income arising from deposits, bills, or debt instruments held before the entry into force of the Amendment Act (i.e., before 20 August 2019).[21]

---

[21] See KPMG Thailand. 2019. Thailand Tax Updates.

X

Recent Developments and Future Direction

A. Recent Major Developments

Recent major developments are considered those that occurred in the bond or capital market in Thailand since the publication of the *ASEAN+3 Bond Market Guide Thailand* in August 2016. For easy reference, the developments are reflected in descending chronological order.

1. Issuance of the First Corporate Social Bond (2021) [NEW]

In November 2021, the Thai bond market witnessed the first issuance of a social bond by a non-financial institution issuer under the ASEAN social bond standards. The 5-year bond issued by Thaifoods Group is believed to also be the first nonfinancial corporate social bond in any ASEAN market. The sustainable finance framework of the company is available from the issuer's website.

2. Introduction of Bond Investor Registration (2021) [NEW]

The BOT and the SEC jointly introduced the BIR scheme in April 2021. The BIR represents an electronic registration system for nonresidents investing in debt securities and is aimed at improving information on foreign investment flows. Nonresident investors, as well as resident investors in a later phase of the scheme, need to obtain a BIR at the UBO level of the debt securities, typically via their custodian.

The introduction of the BIR concept aims to enhance data quality at the UBO level in terms of the accuracy, coverage, and timeliness of bond market activities to support timely and targeted policy measures to safeguard financial stability. The BIR is also part of the BOT's plan to improve the monitoring and effectiveness of foreign exchange surveillance and management policy under the new foreign exchange ecosystem development initiative. A summary document on the new policy framework is available from the BOT website.[22]

Please see Chapter II.M for more information on the BIR.

3. First Sustainability Bond issued by the Government of Thailand (2020) [NEW]

In August 2020, the PDMO successfully issued Thailand's first sustainability bond, with the use of proceeds aimed at financing green infrastructure and social impact projects. The issuance follows the introduction of Thailand's *Sustainable Financing Framework* 1 month earlier.

---

[22] See https://www.bot.or.th/English/MonetaryPolicy/MonetPolicyComittee/MPR/BOX_MRP /BOX4MPR_BOTDevelopFX.pdf.

Please see Chapter III.B for more details on government sustainability bonds and their purposes.

4.   Publication of Sustainable Financing Framework (2020) [NEW]

In July 2020, the Government of Thailand published its *Sustainable Financing Framework*. The framework defines eligible areas for the use of proceeds from green and social bond issuance, prescribes specific exclusions, the process for project evaluation and selection, the management of proceeds, and reporting.

The framework is aligned with the Green Bond Principles, Social Bond Principles, and Sustainability Bond Guidelines published by the ICMA, as well as the ASEAN Green Bond Standards, ASEAN Social Bond Standards, and ASEAN Sustainability Bond Standards. The framework is also aligned with the Green Loan Principles issued by the Loan Market Association.

The Government of Thailand's *Sustainable Financing Framework* as well as periodic verification opinion are available in English from the PDMO website.[23]

5.   Introduction of Blockchain Platform for Government Savings Bonds (2020) [NEW]

On 26 August 2020, the BOT successfully issued THB50 billion of government savings bonds to retail investors in digital form, marking the launch of its new blockchain issuance platform. The new platform was aimed at increasing issuance efficiency and cutting down on the distribution timeframe for new issuances.

The initiative, referred to as the DLT Scripless Bond Project, represented a collaborative effort between the BOT, PDMO, Thailand Securities Depository Co., Ltd, ThaiBMA, and four domestic banks.

Following a successful implementation of the blockchain solution, the BOT plans to expand issuance via the platform to all other government bond types aimed at both retail and wholesale investors.

Chapter III.E contains further detail on the government blockchain issuance platform and the bond types now available on the platform.

6.   Development of Digital Infrastructure Project [2019] [NEW]

In September 2019, the SEC launched an initiative to develop new digital infrastructure for the capital market that aims to connect all capital market participants, cover all fundamental activities from issuance to settlement, and support all capital market products (i.e., bonds, investment units, and equities). This initiative utilizes DLT to help transform all capital-market-related activities from their traditional operation to a complete digital infrastructure that enhances the overall efficiency of capital market services, minimizes the need for reconciliation and manual data verification, reduces risk and cost across processes for participants, enables greater transparency in business transactions, and helps regulators to quickly detect and respond to market anomalies.

This project received financial support from the Capital Market Development Fund. The digital infrastructure services were developed and are operated by the designated operator in collaboration with the Thai Bankers Association, Association of Thai Securities Companies, and Stock Exchange of Thailand. This project has already been approved

---

[23] See https://www.pdmo.go.th/pdmomedia/documents/2020/Jul/KOT%20Sustainable%20Financing%20Framework.pdf.

by the Ministry of Finance and was recognized under the Third Thai Capital Market Development Plan, 2017–2021.

Currently, there are 36 market participants (both issuers and intermediaries) that have joined the project under the SEC sandbox and are developing their internal systems to support connectivity to the digital infrastructure. The first live phase will focus on corporate bonds in 2022, with the intention to further develop the digital infrastructure needed to support government infrastructure bonds and other products.

Please see Chapter III.E for more details on bond issuance via DLT platforms in Thailand.

7.   Adjustment to the Measures to Prevent Thai Baht Speculation (2019) [NEW]

In July 2019, the BOT lowered the amount that daily Thai baht balance nonresident account holders are able to maintain across all cash accounts with domestic financial institutions from THB300 million to THB200 million.

Chapter II.M has more information on the details of the adjustment and other related measures to prevent Thai baht speculation implemented by the BOT.

8.   Sustainable Finance Initiative (2018) [NEW]

The SEC introduced a regulation to allow issuance of green, social, and sustainability bonds in late 2018. This marked the first step to promote sustainable bond market development in Thailand.

The SEC considered that sustainable debt instruments were not new types of instruments but rather were debt instruments with specific use of proceeds related to projects that contribute to positive environmental and social outcomes. Therefore, existing regulations applicable to issuance of debt securities were used to supervise the issuer of such sustainable debt securities in addition to the requirement to comply with international standards and practices. To further develop the capital market's key role in contributing to solving social and environmental issues and promoting sustainable development of businesses in various industries more extensively through the alternative sustainable finance product, the SEC has issued regulations related to issuance and offer for sale of SLBs in May 2021. Similar to green, social, and sustainability bonds, these SLB regulations are in accordance with internationally recognized standards and also made reference to conventional debt securities regulations.[24]

9.   Changes to the Private Placement to Accredited Investors Regime (2018) [NEW]

Effective 1 April 2018, the SEC revised the types of issuance and offerings of debt securities via private placement from the original PP-AI concept into a distinction between offers to institutional investors and offers to HNWs.[25] Both types of investors had been part of the original definition of Accredited Investors (professional investors) published by the SEC in 2009. The actual definition of professional investors remained unchanged.

---

[24] See Resource Center for Sustainable Development Bonds. Laws and Regulations. https://www.sec.or.th/TH/Pages/LAWANDREGULATIONS/RESOURCECENTER.aspx.
[25] Private Placement Scheme under the Notification of the Capital Market Supervisory Board No. Tor Jor. 17/2561 Re: Application and Approval for Offer for Sale of Newly Issued Debt Securities, effective on 1 April 2018.

The revised scheme differentiates parts of the approval process, credit rating requirements, and post-offering obligations for offers to institutional investors and those to HNWs. In addition, the latest scheme makes offers to both institutional investors and HNWs eligible to be issued under the MTN program introduced by the SEC at the same time (see also item 10).

Details of the changes from PP-AI to the latest private placement issuance and offering scheme, and a comparison between the private placement issuance types, can be found in Chapter III.E.

10.   Introduction of Bond Issuance Program (2018) [NEW]

After detailed deliberations, the SEC in April 2018 introduced the ability to issue debt securities via an MTN program. The program issuance is available for all issuance forms, whether public offering or private placement, and requires the issuer to actively report material changes to its financial and business conditions during the tenure of the issued bonds.

Chapter III.E contains further details on the program's issuance, while the material change criteria are explained in detail under continuous disclosure requirements in Chapter II.G.

B.   Future Direction

1.   Public Consultation on Regulatory Guillotine Scheme

The SEC recently concluded a public consultation on a regulatory guillotine scheme for bond market regulations.[26] Several changes to regulations can be expected starting from January 2023. According to the SEC, the objectives of the regulatory guillotine scheme are to improve the efficiency and effectiveness of the oversight of debt securities offerings, as well as to reduce the burden on the issuer while maintaining an appropriate level of investor protection. Specifically, the public consultation was aimed at improving debt instrument supervision regulations by (i) reducing the number of regulations granting permission to offer debt securities for sale to a minimum,
(ii) updating the rules to ensure they are consistent with other types of instruments without unduly burdening the debt issuer, and (iii) clarifying and simplifying the rules to create an easy-to-understand regulatory environment. The public consultation paper included the following major items as described below.

a)   Reducing the Number of Regulations Granting Permission to Offer for Sale Debt Securities to a Minimum

There are currently a plethora of rules and regulations governing the approval for sale of debt securities, the majority of which contain similar content. The only difference is in minor details such as currency, issuer type, and instrument type. This creates confusion and redundancy among debt issuers and market participants. Additionally, there was a problem with the inconsistent application of terminology across regulations.

---

[26] The text provided is based on SEC consultation documents available only in the Thai language at https://www.sec.or.th/Documents/PHS/Main/748/hearing322564.pdf. While it has been translated for the purpose of this update note by the ABMF SF1 team, the document may not be available permanently.

The SEC discovered that there are currently 13 regulations governing the offer for sale of debt securities, 11 of which are similar in content and could be consolidated. Additionally, this would facilitate resolving inconsistencies between relevant regulations. The proposed regulation will cover all types of debt instruments issued in Thai baht and in foreign currency in the domestic market.

b)   Updating the Rules to Ensure They Are Consistent with Other Types of Instruments without Unduly Burdening the Debt Issuer

Currently, approval criteria for debt instruments and equity securities are similar, particularly on major issues such as the issuer's financial standards (for public offerings), director and executive qualifications, and prohibited characteristics of the issuer. However, it was discovered that the regulations for both instruments contained inconsistencies in their wording, which could cause difficulties in subsequent interpretation.

Meanwhile, the SEC is also revising its definition of an investor. This will almost certainly have an impact on most of the regulations governing the offer and sale of debt securities. Additionally, certain regulations should be revised to ensure that they are consistent with others. For example, the regulation governing financial institutions' issuance of subordinated debt instruments to meet Basel III regulatory capital requirements does not yet align the issuer's qualifications for an offering to HNWs and the public with those for other debt instruments.

Going forward, the SEC will amend relevant debt instrument regulations to incorporate the SEC's proposed new investor definitions, which will take risk and complexity into account. The definitions of private placements to 10 persons (PP10), institutional investor, ultra-HNW and HNW definitions will be amended. Additionally, the SEC will revise relevant regulations to ensure consistency, such as those governing the offer and sale of Basel III instruments and *sukuk*.

c)   Clarifying and Simplifying the Rules to Create an Easy-to-Understand Regulatory Environment

The SEC will simplify certain rules and regulations to make them more understandable and use plain language to eliminate any ambiguities. For example, the notification of approval for the sale of debt securities contains no information about the approval's validity for domestic issuance. The approval for the sale of equity and debt securities in foreign markets, on the other hand, must be completed within 6 months of the date of approval. As a result, many issuers fail to issue securities even after the SEC has granted approval. To ensure consistency with other comparable regulations and to provide clarity to issuers and their advisors, the SEC will require the issuer to complete the debt securities issuance within 6 months of the approval date (which can be extended once). In the case of an MTN for public offering, the new regulation states that the issuer must meet all requirements for the public offering, even if the initial series under such an MTN program will be offered to institutional investors. For example, the issuer is required to appoint an intermediary, even though that is not required under current regulations if the first series of the MTN program is offered to institutional investors.

While the SEC is revising its definition of an investor, it is also considering revising certain requirements under the current PP10 regime to ease the burden on issuers. As a result, the SEC intends to make fundraising easier for issuers by exempting PP10 offerings from the following criteria: (i) an issuer with no history of mismanagement of the use of proceeds within the preceding 2 years prior to the date of application submission, and (ii) the submission of a resolution of the shareholders' meeting or the board of directors prior to the offering of debt securities.

To accommodate the changing market environment and to increase investor protection, the SEC is considering providing clarity on the issuance process for secured bonds and the use of collateral. At the moment, debt instruments can be collateralized by the issuer's assets or a legally enforceable guarantee that must be maintained throughout the life of the debt instrument and is specified exclusively for the public offering. The SEC believes, however, that it is appropriate to expand the collateral feature applicable to both HNWs and public offerings to reduce the risk of collateral being lost if the issuer experiences financial difficulties or defaults on payments. According to the consultation paper, when collateral is used, this does not include the issuer's shares. When a guarantee is required, the guarantor must be a legal entity. Additionally, the SEC intends to prohibit the use of guarantor ratings in lieu of issue ratings in the public offering of long-term debt securities. According to the SEC, issue ratings provide investors with accurate and comprehensive information that aids in their decision-making.

The SEC is considering simplifying the issuance process of structured notes. At present, there are different rules and regulations governing the issuance of structured notes by various types of issuers. This adds complexity and confusion to the market, which may result in unintentional violations of rules and regulations. In light of this, the SEC is considering extending the approval period for structured notes issued by financial institutions to 2 years. These products can be offered to all types of investors and include both short- and long-term securities. This 2-year period is consistent with current regulations that permit corporations and limited companies to sell structured notes to the general public. Meanwhile, the filing document for structured notes will be consolidated into a single form, Form 69-SN. This form will be divided into two sections: (i) Form SN-1, which will contain information about the issuer, including the characteristics of the initial issue; and (ii) Form SN-2, which will contain additional characteristics and any material changes in the issuer's status. When capital-protected structured notes are offered for sale to the general public, an issuer rating or guarantor rating is required to provide investors with additional information for making investment decisions.

The SEC proposes that an announcement on the above will take effect concurrently with the implementation of the new investor definitions, which are currently under development and expected to be implemented within 2022.

Appendix 2
Resource Information

For easy reference and access to further information about the topics discussed in this update note, interested parties are encouraged to utilize the following links (all websites available in English); items marked 'NEW' were not included in the *ASEAN+3 Bond Market Guide for Thailand* or have since changed:

ASEAN Capital Markets Forum—ASEAN Green Bond Standards [NEW]
https://www.theacmf.org/initiatives/sustainable-finance/asean-green-bond-standards.

ASEAN+3 Bond Market Guide—Thailand (2016)
https://asianbondsonline.adb.org/abmg.php#tha-2016.

AsianBondsOnline (Asian Development Bank) [NEW]
https://asianbondsonline.adb.org/economy/?economy=TH.

AsianBondsOnline (Asian Development Bank)—Green Bonds [NEW]
https://asianbondsonline.adb.org/green-bonds/index.html.

Bank of Thailand—Bond Investor Registration [NEW]
https://www.bot.or.th/English/FinancialMarkets/Pages/BIR-Eng.aspx.

Climate Bonds Initiative [NEW]
https://www.climatebonds.net.

Government of Thailand Sustainable Financing Framework [NEW]
https://www.pdmo.go.th/pdmomedia/documents/2020/Jul/KOT%20Sustainable%20Financing%20Framework.pdf

Green Bond Principles (International Capital Market Association) [NEW]
https://www.icmagroup.org/green-social-and-sustainability-bonds/green-bond-principles-gbp/..

Public Debt Management Office of the Ministry of Finance of Thailand
http://www.pdmo.go.th/en/.

Thai Bond Market Association
https://www.thaibma.or.th/EN/homeen.aspx.

Thai Bond Market Association—Green, Social, Sustainability Bond, and Sustainability-Linked Bonds Webpage [NEW]
https://www.thaibma.or.th/EN/BondInfo/ESG.aspx.

The Securities and Exchange Commission, Thailand—Debt Securities
https://www.sec.or.th/EN/Pages/LawandRegulations/DebtInstrument.aspx.

Appendix 3
Glossary of Technical Terms

This glossary focuses on terms that appear in this update note.

blockchain	Digital ledger of transactions [NEW]
Bond Investor Registration	Registration concept for investors in the Thai bond market [NEW]
consideration period	Decision and approval timeframe stipulated by the Securities and Exchange Commission, Thailand (SEC)
green bond	Bond that raises proceeds for environmental (green) projects or those aimed at combating climate change [NEW]
Green Bond Principles	A set of rules and criteria for designating a green bond; developed and maintained by the International Capital Market Association [NEW]
institutional investors	Professional investor concept in the Thai bond market
Nonresident Baht Account	Cash account in Thai baht to be maintained by nonresident investors
Nonresident Baht Account for Securities	Designated cash account for nonresident investors in securities
observation period	Due diligence and review period stipulated by the SEC
private placement	Method of issuance not through a public offering, with specific eligibility for issuing entities and limitation of investor types
prospectus	Key disclosure document for a public offer for sale of bonds
public offer	Issuance of securities under the public offer issuance concept
registration	Refers to the registration of debt securities with the Thai Bond Market Association
registration statement	Key document to be submitted for approval to the SEC
social bond	Bonds with proceeds exclusively applied to finance or raise funds for new and existing projects with positive social outcomes [NEW]
Segregated Securities Account	Securities account to be opened at ultimate beneficial owner level by nonresident investors in bonds [NEW]
sustainability bond	Bond that raises proceeds for environmental (green) and social projects [NEW]
transfer restrictions	Statement by the issuer to the SEC that the bonds may only be sold and transferred to professional investors

| sustainability-linked bond | Sustainability-linked bonds are any type of bond instrument for which the financial and/or structural characteristics can vary depending on whether the issuer achieves predefined sustainability or environmental, social, and governance objectives [NEW] |

Source: ASEAN+3 Bond Market Forum Sub-Forum 1 team.